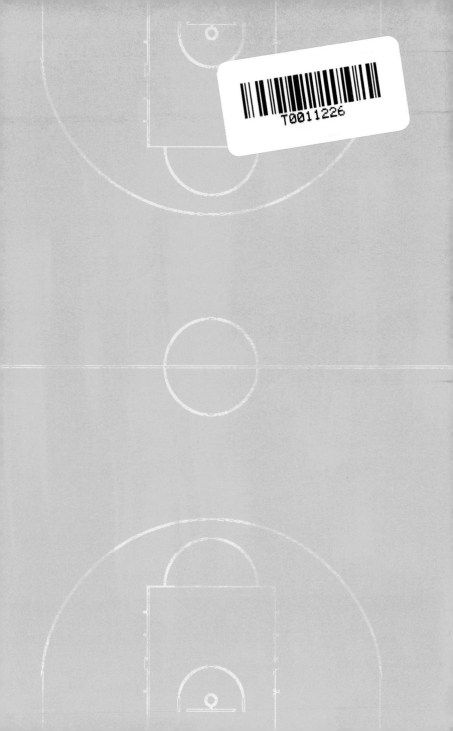

OP
P
GS 2

New Royalty

Charles R. Smith Jr.

CANDLEWICK PRESS

CONTENTS

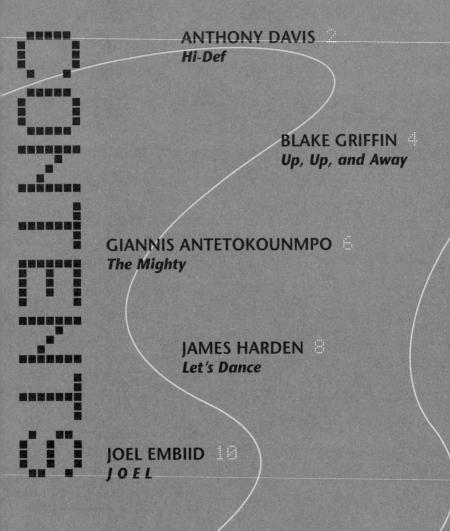

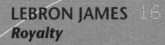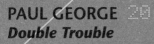

Hi-Def

ANTHONY DAVIS

AD
in HD,
Hi-Def,
he be
quicker
faster
bigger
stronger,
better handle
better hops
with a wingspan much longer,
and taller
way taller,
showing the skill set
of a baller
much smaller.
Jump shots
dime drops
crossovers
and shakes
and rim-rocking finishes
after leading the break,
all part of the upgrade,
Baller 2.0,
AD in HD
putting on a show.

Up, Up, Away

Buckle your seat belts
cleared for takeoff,
Blake Griffin on the runway
ready to liftoff.

Flight BG 23
on the fast break
building up speed
to rise and elevate
soar and accelerate,
wheels up
wings out
up up goes Blake.

Ball in hand
held up high
Air Griffin rises
rises to fly
higher
and higher
and higher
through the sky.

Up
up
and away
goes Blake
then drops through the clouds
to slam home the fast break.

and

BLAKE
GRIFFIN

ghty

GIANNIS ANTETOKOUNMPO

Blessed by the gods
with warrior gifts,
a mortal rises to become
the Mighty Giannis.

Feet of Hermes,
vision of Artemis,
artistry of Apollo,
strength of Hephaestus.
Cool
confident
calm demeanor
and warrior spirit
of the goddess Athena.

Rage of Ares,
power of Poseidon,
the Mighty Giannis
STRIKES
like Zeus with lightning!

et's D

Shimmy
shake
spin
stride
dribble in
step back
dribble out
slide
to the right
to the left
to the right
again,
dribble left
dribble left
step
spin.
Dribble in
step back
defender falls
dribble stop.

Stare down
rise up
let fly
watch drop.

JAMES
HARDEN

J
uggernaut

O_f

**O**_f

E
xtreme

L
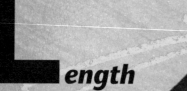ength

JOEL
EMBIID

KD B-B

KEVIN
DURANT

a

KD B-ball
he ball
all the time.
KD do it all
with the ball
all the time.

Seven foot
fast break
KD
no brakes
crosses over
hesitates
stutter-steps
ankles break
throws it down
shimmy-shakes.

KD be balling,
he ball
all the time.
KD do it all
with the ball
all the time.
Crunch time
clutch time
KD
time to shine.
Toes behind
three-point line
wrist flick
touch twine.

All-Star,
Olympian,
scoring champ,
MVP.
KD be ball.
B-ball be KD.

The Am Kyrie

Step right up
step up to see
the Magician with the Ball
the Amazing Kyrie.

Keep your eyes on the ball
keep your eyes on Kyrie
now you see him, now you don't
do you trust what you see?

KYRIE
IRVING

One defender
two defender
three defenders stand
before Kyrie as he
performs sleight of hand.

Can Kyrie escape
the three-man wall?
Can Kyrie escape
to score the basketball?

Step left
cross right
cross back
out of sight.
Past defenders
behind the back
take it strong
to the rack
defender falls
with a crack!

Now, for the grand finale,
such a sight to see,
can Kyrie go
coast to coast to victory?
Dribble slow
dribble slow
cross over
then go,
faster and faster
Kyrie dribbling,
crossing
and turning
and swerving
and spinning
until Kyrie
comes to a stop
behind the three-point line
then lets it pop
with no time left
as the ball drops,
giving his team
a victory
from the magical hand
of the Amazing Kyrie!

Royalt

Ladies and gentlemen, welcome
to the court of basketball.
It is my privilege to present to you
a giant who stands tall:
the Fearless Prince
Emperor of Improvisation,
the Marquess of Finesse
the Earl of Elevation.
The Viscount of Vision
Archduke of the Assist
tossing ten pence to teammates
with a flick of the wrist.
The Baron of the Chase Block
with the one-hand swoop,
Lord of the Leap,
Sir Alley
of the Oop.

His Royal Highness rising
high over the hoop,
the Ruler of the Rim
looking down on the hoop,
the Duke of Disrespectful Dunks
destroying the hoop.
The Monarch of Mid-Range and Long
with the feather-soft touch,
hailing from the Land of Cleve,
the Count of Clutch
etching his name
in legendary games,
the exalted one,
the royal
King James.

**LEBRON
JAMES**

The Legend of Luka

Once upon a time
in a land far away,
Slovenia, to be exact,
lived a boy who loved to play,
a boy named Luka
and Luka loved to play
the game of basketball
all the time
every day.

Luka played with passion
skill
and joy
and soon earned the nickname
Wonderboy.
Then at age thirteen
Wonderboy left for Spain
just to play basketball,
to eat, sleep, and train,
and by the age of sixteen
Wonderboy turned pro,
the third youngest ever
to be a EuroLeague pro,
a boy among men
still continuing to grow.

LUKA
DONČIĆ

end

So
the legend of Luka
grew game after game
with Wonderboy showing
how he earned his name:
a jump shot with range
slick ball-handling skill
a mind for basketball
and a champion's will.
Luka's game grew
and so did his size
and soon Luka's name
drew NBA eyes.
At nineteen years old
the EuroLeague MVP,
fresh off a championship,
looked across the sea
to the next challenge
and knew what to do:
show the world
the legend is true.

Double Trouble

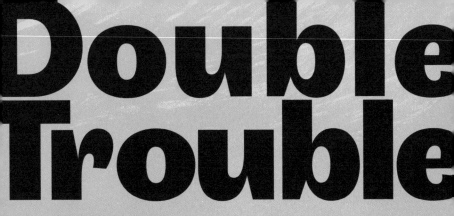

Crouching wide
crouching wide
in his defensive stance,
harassing his man
with fast, active hands,
PG pokes
pokes the ball free.
Another steal
another steal
at the hands of PG!

Turn around
take off
cross half-court line,
dribble
dribble pause,
what's on PG's mind?
Will he shoot the long three?
Dribble in and step back?
Flip up a floater
or take it to the rack?
PG explodes
explodes
on the attack,
racing
rising
then rattling the rim
with thunder echoing
throughout the gym.
Defense
to offense,
making it look easy,
Double
Trouble
PG
be.

PAUL
GEORGE

21

Freak o Nature

Racing
and rumbling
and whistling
it comes
like lightning
crackling
the air
here it comes.
Twisting
and turning
and gusting
it comes
kicking up dust
here it comes
here it comes.
Shifting
and spinning
and rocking
and shaking
defenders to the ground
before elevating,

take cover
take cover
here it comes
here it comes.
Rising
higher
than rain clouds fly,
look out,
it's here
striking down from the sky
landing with thunder
destroying the rim
with the earth-shaking force
of the Westbrook Wind!

RUSSELL
WESTBROOK

2 Many Names

Stepping on the court
representing number 30,
honoring his dad,
the baby-faced Steph Curry
human highlight every night
in a hurry Steph Curry.

Chameleon
changing up his game,
shooting passing scoring
taking on many names:
the Chef
the Technician
the Maestro
the Magician
the Video Game Character
with Dead-Eye Precision.

Slippery Steph
with the ball going left
with the skip
with the slip
with the shimmy
with the dip
with the hesi
                    hesi
                          tation
to the finger-roll flip.

The whirling dervish
impervious to defenders
sending opponents home
with buzzer-beating finishers.

The Warrior
with an eagle eye,
lock in from long distance
anytime and let it fly
with a flick of the wrist
touch twine
point to sky.

The Chef cooking
with the spice in his game
with the fire in his heart
with the ice in his veins
feeds crowds with a mouthful
of too many names.

STEPHEN CURRY

ZOOM 2.5

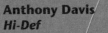

Anthony Davis
Hi-Def

No one represents the new type of player better than Anthony Davis. He plays like a much smaller player even though he is almost seven feet tall. Since he's doing things unseen before, I decided to compare him to a high-tech TV, with all its bigger and better features. Technology is always advancing, so I call him version 2.0, an upgrade over other players. He is often called AD, and high-definition TV is often called HD. The two rhyme, so it was a perfect fit.

Blake Griffin
Up, Up, and Away

One of the more veteran players represented in the book, Blake made a lot of noise in the league when he entered by flying OVER players and doing dunk-contest-style dunks in actual games. I wanted to show how high he could get, so I compared him to an airplane and wrote about a flight from takeoff to landing.

Giannis Antetokounmpo
The Mighty

Since Giannis was born and raised in Greece, I wanted to compare him to something the Greeks are known for: the gods and goddesses of Greek mythology. Many of them have unique powers, so I decided to show what skills he was given by the various gods in the pantheon.

James Harden
Let's Dance

Certain players are known for certain moves, and James Harden is known for his step-back jump shot. I wanted to center his poem around that, so I imagined him dancing to music as he tries to shake his man to set up the shot.

Joel Embiid
J O E L

Joel is known not just for his unique skill set as a big man; he also has one of the longest wingspans and some of the biggest hands in the NBA. I kept his poem simple by connecting his extreme size to his name. I'm also a big fan of comic books, and one of my favorite villains from the Marvel universe is the Juggernaut. His power is that he can run through anything and is unstoppable. Joel is very strong and plays like he is unstoppable.

Kevin Durant
KD B-Ball

When I sat down to write Kevin's poem, all I could think about was how versatile his game is. He can grab the rebound, push the ball up court, and then throw it down. He can also shoot the lights out from deep, but what people don't realize is how tall he is, at just under seven feet. If he were playing years ago, he would have had to play under the basket and not been the same player. I focused on his varied skill set to show he is a complete player and great representative of the game of basketball. I used jazz rhythms in the rhyme pattern because his style is so smooth and easy.

27

Kyrie Irving
The Amazing Kyrie

When a player can handle the ball well, they are said to have the ball on a string. Some players not only have the ball on a string; the great ones can make it move like magic. As I watched Kyrie, I realized he's a magician on the court, making the ball or himself disappear with ease, leaving his defenders looking silly.

LeBron James
Royalty

LeBron is often called King James, so I wanted to play off that idea, putting my own spin on it. I decided to use as many royal and noble titles as I could to connect to his game. I wrote the poem as if he is being introduced among other royalty, with trumpets announcing his presence. I imagined this taking place in medieval times, so I used language to reflect that. For instance, I used the old English term "ten pence" instead of the modern English word *dime*.

Luka Dončić
The Legend of Luka

Luka took the NBA by storm as a rookie. He was born to play the game. Since he came from Europe and made his mark initially in the EuroLeague, I wanted to show his journey to the NBA, telling it as a fairy tale, even though it's all true.

Paul George
Double Trouble

It took a while to figure out what Paul George does especially well because the question was, What doesn't he do well? He can truly do everything. That means offense AND defense. A player that can do both at a high level is Double Trouble, so I focused on showing both in one play.

Russell Westbrook
Freak of Nature

The first thing I noticed about Russell Westbrook is how explosive he is on the court. He runs faster, jumps faster, and goes higher than most players and plays with such intensity that I decided, in his poem, to compare him to a storm. But since he's such a unique player, I made the storm a combination of the mightiest types of weather and named it after him.

Stephen Curry
2 Many Names

The idea behind Steph's poem came simply from trying to figure out what nickname I could start with. As I sat and watched his numerous highlights, I kept saying to myself, "I don't know what to call him—he's got too many names." So instead of fighting it, I embraced it and went with all the names that came to mind.

Dedicated to my son Sebastian and other athletes
who draw inspiration from these great players

First paperback edition 2024

Library of Congress Catalog Card Number 2021946450
ISBN 978-1-5362-1035-4 (hardcover)
ISBN 978-1-5362-3612-5 (paperback)

23 24 25 26 27 28 CCP 10 9 8 7 6 5 4 3 2 1

Printed in Shenzhen, Guangdong, China

This book was typeset in Stone Sans.
Digital artwork and typography by Jason Lin.

Candlewick Press
99 Dover Street
Somerville, Massachusetts 02144

www.candlewick.com

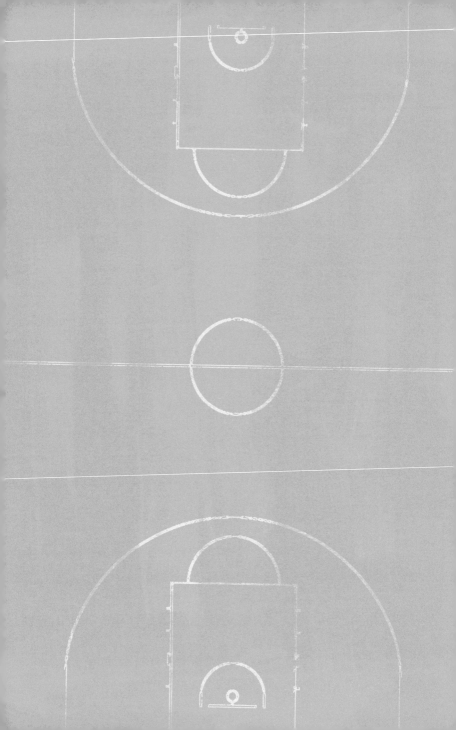

Pass it over to the ladies!

"Pure pleasure for basketball fans and inspiration for kids who doubted poetry was alive, this book . . . is 'all that.'" —*School Library Journal*

Available in paperback

www.candlewick.com

Available in hardcover and as an e-book

Another slam dunk from the pros!

A new generation of WNBA superstars from Sue Bird to Brittney Griner shine bright in this exuberant collection of poems.

It's a whole new ball game!

Churn and burn and fly with these current and past female soccer stars, from Rose Lavelle to Megan Rapinoe, in thirteen new rapid-fire poems.

poems by
Charles R. Smith Jr.
Coretta Scott King Award Winner

Available in hardcover and as an e-book

www.candlewick.com